I Want to Be a BALD EAGLE

by Thomas Kingsley Troupe

Illustrated by Christina Ann Rodriguez

raintree

a Capstone company — publishers for children

I wanted to read one more chapter before breakfast, but Lily and Benji were too loud.

"Pine cone bombs!" Benji shouted. A big pine cone bounced off my head.

"You're a pine tree now, Heather!" Lily said, laughing.

"Perfect," I said.

"I bet it's nice and quiet up there in the clouds," I whispered to myself. "I want to be a bald eagle."

I put down my book. I stood up and felt my body transform!

I rocketed up into the sky, flapping my mighty wings. Wind rushed past my beak and whisked through my feathers. I was flying!

Bald eagles love lakes — the bigger the better! They are often spotted soaring above lakes or perched in lakeside trees. From there, they can spot fish and small animals.

I glided towards a nest in a tall pine tree. I thought it was mine!

The nest was gigantic, even bigger than a bath. I landed on a branch and broke some sticks free with my hooked beak. I stuck them into my nest to make it stronger.

"Hey!" called an eagle near by. She had brown feathers all over, except for her head and tail, which were white. Her talons and beak were yellow, like mine.

"Who are you?" she asked. "What are you doing here?"

"I'm Heather," I said. "I'm just visiting."

The other eagle was called Ella. She seemed a bit scary at first, but she let me stay.

Eagles usually live alone. Pairs come together for nesting, but they don't always stay together year-round. They also don't like other eagles coming into their territory.

She said, "I've got a nest full of screaming babies back at home. They're always hungry."

"Well then, let's hunt!" I said.

Ella and I leaped from the nest into the open air. It was amazing up there. I could see everything!

Baby eagles are called eaglets.

My eyesight was amazing. I saw a fish swimming near a fishing boat. The fish tasted the bait but didn't bite.

"Do your babies like fish?" I asked.

"Of course," Ella said.

I swooped down to the water. It felt like being in the front seat of a roller coaster, but even faster! I bet I was going nearly 160 kilometres (100 miles) per hour!

I snatched the fish up with my talons. The people fishing shouted and shook their fists at me.

Bald eagles are skilled hunters, but sometimes they steal their food. They take food from other predators. They also pick at dead animals they find.

I clutched the fish as I soared above the forest. The fish felt slimy and wet in my talons but I thought Ella's babies would love it.

I watched another eagle far below. It caught a rabbit running through the grass. The poor thing never had a chance!

I also saw Ella pulling meat from a dead raccoon. I couldn't imagine eating that! I hoped the baby eagles weren't fussy.

Ella's babies were screeching like little monsters. They ate the raccoon meat and squawked, begging for more. They were covered in dark feathers, and their beaks were dark too. They didn't look much like bald eagles!

As Ella fed her babies the fish, I watched two fledglings fly. In minutes they were far off in the distance.

"Aren't you worried about them?" I asked.

"They'll be back," Ella said. "But soon they'll fly away for good. They grow up so quickly."

Bald eagles normally lay two or three eggs. Egg-hungry predators usually stay away. The parents are almost always at the nest and ready to protect their eggs!

I flew off to enjoy the view. Billy, a male eagle, flew towards me. I soared in his direction to show I wasn't scared. We clasped our talons together. Then we fell from the sky!

Sometimes a bald eagle will "talon clasp" with another eagle. This dangerous stunt is how some bald eagles show that they're the boss of their territory.

"Are you going to let go?" Billy asked.

"Nope," I said. I was getting dizzy as we fell. "Are you?"

At the last second, he let go and we both flew off, laughing.

That was exciting!

Billy and I soared peacefully on the high winds.

"My grandad died yesterday," Billy said.

"I'm sorry," I said. "How old was he?"

"Almost 27," Billy said. "Pretty old for a bald eagle."

"Grandad remembered when there were only a few bald eagles left," Billy said. "He was afraid we would die out."

"You mean become extinct?" I asked.

"That's right," Billy said. "But it's better now. Humans aren't allowed to harm eagles. They're also stopping some of the pollution that was hurting eagles."

Bald eagles can live for up to 30 years in the wild. Their biggest threats are pollution and loss of their habitats.

My parents were calling, so I said goodbye to Billy.
I flew towards the campsite. In seconds, I was back in
my chair again. It was like I'd never left.

When I stood up, an eagle feather fell from my shoulder.

"Hey," Lily shouted. "Heather's got a feather!"

"That rhymes!" Benji said and they both giggled.

I laughed and smiled up at the bald eagles in the sky.

Once there were fewer than 500 nesting pairs of bald eagles left in the continental United States, which doesn't include Alaska and Hawaii. Now there are more than 10,000 nesting pairs in the same area.

More about bald eagles

- A bald eagle swallows a fish head first so that the spines don't get caught in its throat.

- The bald eagle is found only in North America.

- Some bald eagle nests can weigh as much as 1 tonne!

- Bald eagles can float, and will sometimes use their wings to row across the water.

- While flying, the bald eagle rarely flaps its wings. Instead it soars like a glider, keeping its wings flat.

- Young bald eagles, or fledglings, are able to fly from the nest when they are about 11 weeks old.

- Eagle feathers are protected by US laws. If a feather is on the ground, it can be admired and touched, but must be left where it is.

Glossary

eaglet baby eagle

extinct no longer living; an extinct animal is one that has died out, with no more of its kind left alive

fledgling young bird that is learning to fly

gigantic very big

habitat natural place and conditions in which a plant or animal lives

illegal against the law

predator animal that hunts other animals for food

squawk make a loud, harsh screech

talon sharp, pointed claw on an eagle's toe; each foot has four talons

territory area of land that an animal claims as its own to live in

Read more

Birds (Animal Classification), Angela Royston (Raintree, 2015)

Eagles and Birds of Prey (DK Eyewitness Books), Jemima Parry-Jones (Dorling Kindersley, 2000)

Soaring Eagles (Walk on the Wild Side), Charlotte Guillain (Raintree, 2013)

Websites

www.bbc.co.uk/nature/life/Sea_eagle
Learn about sea-eagles, where they live, what they eat and so much more!

www.dkfindout.com/uk/animals-and-nature/birds/eagles/
Improve your knowledge of bald eagles through fun facts and photographs.

Index

Books in this series

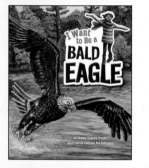

Raintree is an imprint of Capstone Global Library Limited, a company incorporated in England and Wales having its registered office at 7 Pilgrim Street, London, EC4V 6LB – Registered company number: 6695582

www.raintree.co.uk
myorders@raintree.co.uk

Text © Capstone Global Library Limited 2016
The moral rights of the proprietor have been asserted.

Edited by Shelly Lyons and Nick Healy
Designed by Sarah Bennett
Creative Director: Nathan Gassman
Production by Tori Abraham

ISBN 978 1 4747 0423 6
19 18 17 16 15
10 9 8 7 6 5 4 3 2 1

British Library Cataloguing in Publication Data
A full catalogue record for this book is available from the British Library.

Acknowledgements
The illustrations in this book were painted with oil colours.
The photographs on pages 20-21 are reproduced with permission of: Shutterstock/cvrestan, page 21: Shutterstock/S.R. Maglione

We would like to thank the staff at the National Eagle Center in Wabasha, Minnesota, USA, for their expterise, research and advice.

Every effort has been made to contact copyright holders of material reproduced in this book. Any omissions will be rectified in subsequent printings if notice is given to the publisher.

All the internet addresses (URLs) given in this book were valid at the time of going to press. However, due to the dynamic nature of the internet, some addresses may have changed, or sites may have changed or ceased to exist since publication. While the author and publisher regret any inconvenience this may cause readers, no responsibility for any such changes can be accepted by either the author or the publisher.

Printed in China.